This book is designed to provide
information is provided and sold with
publisher and author do not offer any legal or other professional advice. In the case of a need for any such expertise consult with the appropriate professional. This book does not contain all information available on the subject. This book has not been created to be specific to any individual's or organizations' situation or needs. Every effort has been made to make this book as accurate as possible. However, there may be typographical and or content errors. Therefore, this book should serve only as a general guide and not as the ultimate source of subject information. This book contains information that might be dated and is intended only to educate and entertain. The author and publisher shall have no liability or responsibility to any person or entity regarding any loss or damage incurred, or alleged to have incurred, directly or indirectly, by the information contained in this book.

What are Kindle Quickreads?

Kindle Quickreads are a series of short books that are meant to be read in one sitting. Each "Quickread" tackles just one particular subject. This series of books aims to give readers the encouragement, assistance and ideas they need to handle specific problems or areas of personal growth.

Kindle Quickreads are exclusive to Amazon's Kindle platform. They are not available for purchase or borrow in any other format. They may be downloaded on Kindle devices or read utilizing the Kindle app on your phone, computer or tablet.

Various talented authors have contributed to the Kindle Quickread series and our team continues to grow. Their talents and insights have helped thousands of people and we look forward to offering many additional books in this series over the coming months.

In this edition of the Kindle Quickread series, Daria Foster is going to show us the benefits of decuttering and why there is great value to minimizing our mess.

Invest more in relationships than possessions.

Invest more in relationships than possessions.

Before we dig into some practical suggestions to help you declutter and minimize your mess, let me first address an often overlooked aspect of this subject.

Unnecessary accumulation creates clutter. It's a simple concept, but the fact is that you don't consider that concept every time you make an unnecessary purchase. Clutter gathers over time, and before you know it, things you've bought are getting in the way of your everyday life. The sheer magnitude of the work involved in organizing and decluttering is daunting sometimes, but there are ways to minimize the stuff you're going to need to clean up later on. And more than discipline, it's really a matter of perspective.

It's very easy to get caught up in consumerism. It's even easier to get attached to the stuff you buy. When you make a purchase with your hard-earned money, you feel like you deserve it — and that's completely understandable. The caveat is that not every thing you buy enriches and enhances your life. That's why most of them end up as clutter, which really does the opposite.

Whenever you're in a store considering a purchase, ask yourself three things:

- *Will this improve or enhance my life in ways that justify its price?*

- *Is this the best place to spend my money?*

- *Will postponing this purchase be an unwise decision?*

If you answer yes to all of these questions, then you can go through with the purchase. Otherwise, there are better things to do with your money. Do as much research as you can. Make sure you're getting the best deal. Whether it's a watch or a car, practice due diligence when it comes to spending your hard-earned money.

An obvious, and easily overlooked, suggestion is to save it. Big savings can account for bigger, better, and wiser financial decisions whether those are investments or purchases. Chances are, the longer you wait, the more thought you will be giving to the things you buy.

It's also wise to step back and take a look at your life every once in a while. This involves not only introspection but the physical act of checking your accounts and transactions to see where your money goes. Be aware of your consumer habits. Do you buy cheap things, but often? Or do you make big purchases you don't have an immediate need for? All these result in you being cash-strapped whenever a need or a greater desire does come up.

Most importantly, ask yourself if you're spending your money on the things that matter. Do you miss trips with your loved ones because you had spent all your earnings on clothes? Are you still able to go to the occasional brunch to catch up with your friends? Do you have financial security for your family, especially the children?

At the end of the day, money matters, but where you put it matters even more. Spend it enriching your life with love, joy, and strong relationships. This helps you avoid physical clutter in your home and at the same time build happy human connections. You can regret buying an expensive purse that didn't evolve with your style, but quality time and great relationships with people are much harder concerns to be regretful about.

Establish and enforce a proper "home" for what you own.

Establish and enforce a proper "home" for what you own.

It has been a bummer of a day at work and you're looking forward to having a relaxing night watching TV while gobbling down your dinner. You're also excited at the prospect of having a good night's sleep.

But when you get home, all you see is clutter. The house is a mess. Clean and dirty clothes are on the floor and on the couch. Last night's dishes are still on the table. There are lots of action figures scattered around and your beer bottle collection occupying your shelves and gathering dust. Things aren't where they are supposed to be.

Chances are there is so much stuff in your house that you can't even dare call it a home. You tell yourself that no amount of cleaning up can fix this. It's hopeless.

If that's what you think, let me make a few suggestions related to placement and storage. The trick is making sure that everything you own has it's proper "home." The floor isn't it's home. The dining room table isn't it's home. You see where I'm going with this...

1. Organizing your stuff is one thing, decluttering is another. Start off by analyzing everything that you have. Pick up one thing and decide whether it is for throwing away, for donating or selling, or for keeps. Assign a box for each of these and label them KEEP, TOSS, and DONATE. Sometimes, deciding on the spot may be a tad difficult. You can place that thing in a separate box labeled TO BE DECIDED.

2. Decluttering takes time. You can't do the whole house in one day. One technique is to do one room at a time. This will give you a sense of accomplishment every time you finish a room.

3. Once you've decided on the things you want to keep, the next step is to organize. First off, sort out the stuff you've decided to keep. Organize them according to their kind or usage. Clothes belong to the closet in your bedroom. Bed linens and towels should have their own place. Kitchen stuff belong in the kitchen. And your beer bottle collection belongs to the dump or recycling plant. Yep! Get rid of those bottles. You're an adult now. Beer bottles don't have a place in your home anymore.

4. Start finding the perfect place to keep all your stuff. Clear out and clean up those closets, cabinets, and other places you can store your

things in. Imagine what you can put in there.

5. Go out and buy storage bins, boxes, baskets, and the like. Make sure to organize and sort all your stuff first before buying the storage pieces. This is important. You need to know the measurements before you buy them. It's also helpful to buy clear bins for certain items. That way you won't have to search through bin after bin to locate what you're looking for once everything is put away.

6. Invest in furniture with hidden storage compartments. Get yourself some stackable storage bins if you have a large enough space where you can stack them. As much as possible, put all items of a kind in one container. For example, place all your Christmas ornaments in one box, label it, then set it aside where it will stay hidden until the time comes to take it out.

7. Go through the boxes from time to time so you can sort them out once more. You will probably be bringing home more and more stuff as time goes by and you'll need space for these things.

Your home can truly start to feel like a home when everything you own is in it's "home".

Employ the 6-Month Rule to Clothing

Employ the 6-Month Rule to Clothing

You know what the biggest problem with clothes is? People often complain that they don't have enough. How many times have you heard yourself say, "I don't have anything to wear!" Chances are, you have enough in your closet but you just don't wear most of them. It's high time you declutter your wardrobe.

Put everything on the floor and analyze each piece of clothing. Look at each one. Get a feel. Do you like it? Does it look worn out? No and yes? Get rid of it.

Separate your clothes according to season. Group them into the first half and second half of a year. The first half can consist of your winter and spring clothes. The latter half should include your summer wardrobe, including swimsuits and the like, and autumn/fall clothes. Give each group 6 months then see if there are clothes that you didn't wear or wore sporadically during that season. Those need to go.

Does it dredge bad memories? Does it invoke images of you getting dumped by your girlfriend or boyfriend? Is that what you were wearing when you got into a fight? Anything that reminds you of those bad moments needs to go. You don't need the clutter and you certainly don't need the negativity.

Even if you rocked an outfit a few years ago, consider getting rid of it if it's outdated. Styles come and go. That's how fashion works. You don't want to hang on to those worn-out flared jeans even if you consider it part of your family. Some trends can be outdated already and a comeback may not be on the horizon. If you're thinking that you can keep such an item just in case it becomes trendy in the future, STOP! You are decluttering. Get rid of clothes you are not going to wear anytime soon.

Sometimes, it may be a bit too much to handle to go through all your clothes in one day. Choosing the clothes you still want in your wardrobe is a complicated task. What you can do is to organize in stages. Start off with your winter collection, which is most likely taking the most space in your closet. Once you're done, go through all your shirts, then the pants, followed by the shirts, dresses, and so on. One technique in thinning out your wardrobe is to do one kind of clothing at a time.

Deciding what needs to go may be rather difficult. While this should not be the case, sometimes you can't help but be sentimental or frugal. If you're dealing with the latter, consider selling your old clothes if you really need the money.

The best way to know if a dress or any item from your wardrobe is for keeps or for disposal is to wear them. Try on each item in your closet. Imagine you're doing a fashion montage and working the runway. This will be extremely fun. Have friends over or get your spouse or partner to help you decide what looks good on you. Try different combinations and see if you'd like any of them. Ultimately, the decision rests on you. The objective is to declutter.

Decluttering does not necessarily mean throwing away your stuff. You can sell them, as mentioned earlier, or donate them to friends or people who need clothing. Not only are you doing them a favor, but you're also doing yourself one.

As often as possible, choose to "borrow" rather than "buy."

As often as possible, choose to "borrow" rather than "buy."

Becoming a minimalist does not solely entail getting rid of lots of stuff in your home. It is also not just about having less pieces of furniture. Minimalism is also a way of life. And one way you can practice being a minimalist is by not buying stuff. The better alternative is to borrow what you need, when you need it.

Borrowing is indeed a lot better than buying. When you borrow, you refrain from spending on something you really don't need and want. You can save your money for more important things like emergency expenses or bank savings.

When you borrow stuff that has not been used for a long time, you give that item a new lease in life. Oftentimes, things such as tools are forgotten and left inside the garage to gather dust. Do your friend a favor by borrowing stuff from them that they don't use anymore or haven't used for a long time. This will prevent them from getting rusty and unusable in the future.

If your neighbor has a pair of shears that you badly need, why not ask him or her politely if you can use it in exchange for something of yours — say, a lawn mower. You both get to shape your shrubs and mow your lawns. You can take turns if your neighbor is up to it. That way, both of you will get something out of the exchange.

Another alternative is to actually barter with other people. While this is not exactly borrowing, you still don't get to spend money. Through bartering, you can get rid of an item that has no place in your home anymore, for something that you can actually use.

The most important reason why would borrow instead of buy is that you avoid hoarding stuff. If you keep buying things, they usually end up as clutter. When you borrow something, that thing is in your home only during the time you need it. If you're done with it, simply return it to its owner. No need to find a place to store it. No clutter.

When it comes to clothes, many people like to buy a lot. You pass by a store and spot a beautiful dress or suit on the window display, and what do you do? If you can spare the money, you'll often end up going into the store and leaving with bags full of new clothes. And then what happens? You get to wear them once or twice and then they end up in your closet for a long time.

First of all, say no to impulsive buying.

Second, if you can borrow the same clothes from your family or friends, try that first. If you're looking for a specific piece of clothing for a specific event, just borrow one. If you are going skiing, for example, and you don't have the necessary outfit, why not borrow from someone who has what you need?

Do you like books? Or rather LOVE them? It's quite understandable for book lovers to collect books. But in time, your place will be swarming with books such that you don't have enough space to move around in. The solution: Don't buy books. Of course, you can always invest in a Kindle or any gadget that you can read tons of e-books with but for true-blue book lovers, the feel and smell of books add to the experience. To avoid hoarding books, just borrow those you haven't read yet. Simply return them when you're done.

Make ample use of "accordion folders" to avoid living in a disorganized world of paperwork.

Make ample use of "accordion folders" to avoid living in a disorganized world of paperwork.

One of the most common problems when it comes to dealing with clutter is paper. Many are guilty of keeping different kinds of documents and other important and not-so-important stuff that are on paper. Oftentimes, there is just so much paper clutter in the home that you can't find the important documents when you need them. Other times, you just give up looking and simply get new copies. The problem here is the time, money, and effort wasted trying to procure documents that are actually just in your home somewhere. But because of all the clutter, it seems they've been lost a long time ago.

To avoid such problems, some decluttering is of the essence.

The first rule of decluttering paper is NOT to collect paper. In this day and age, everything can be stored in your computer and other gadgets. There are books and there are e-books. Hoarding books in your home may be nice and may give your home that vanilla smell that comes from old books BUT if you have too many, you're probably dealing with space constraints. If you can't have your own library at home, it's better to get an e-library instead. You can keep your old books (after you've sorted them out and gave away those you no longer want to keep) but do not buy new ones. Just download them in your e-book reader.

Now, gather and sort all the paperwork you can find in your home. Most likely, there'll be too much that you'd be tempted to just give up and dump them all back in a drawer or something. To make things a tad easier, do the sorting room by room or area by area.

Be harsh when decluttering. Throw away papers that you don't need. Brochures, invites, old bills, and magazines that you've read a dozen times should be tossed out. A better option is to collect them and take them to the recycling plant or center.

Like with e-book readers, technology can play a major part in your decluttering endeavor. Scan documents and save them in your computer. This way, you still get to keep a copy of the documents, yet you get to lessen your clutter. Whenever you need a copy of that certain document, all you have to do is print out a copy. It's that easy.

For those paperwork that you just can't throw away, you need to organize them. An accordion folder may come in real handy. A filing cabinet will also do the job but one of your goals should be to create more space in your home. Filing cabinets are bulky, noisy when you close and open them, and may turn rusty. Accordion folders are cheaper, easier to handle, and can be stored in boxes or other storage containers.

To start off, gather all the papers and documents that need to be kept. Sort them out. Important personal papers such as birth certificates, marriage licenses, and the like should be kept together. Documents for your car loan, house payment, and others like them should be together, as well. You may also want to keep old drawings and other artworks of your children especially if you are the sentimental kind. Another option is to scan and save them or turn them into posters you can hang onto the wall.

One day each week, pick a room to organize and minimalize.

One day each week, pick a room to organize and minimize.

Getting organized can be daunting, and the word "decluttering" makes even the most seasoned organizers blanch. It's normal to feel overwhelmed the moment you decide to get a handle on the mess in your home, but don't let that feeling stop you! Your efforts will be well worth it, and the sense of fulfillment you'll gain from it will be priceless.

A great strategy is to spread out the work in the span of a week. Decide to tackle one room at a time every day. Once you get started and wake up everyday with a specific objective — for example, to reorganize the kitchen — you'll get into the habit of productivity, and things will get easier. This technique can greatly minimize the stress that comes with having to sort out years' worth of disorganization. There's nothing you can do that'll be more counterproductive than trying to do everything at the same time.

Start with an easy room. This can be different for everyone, depending on where the home's inhabitants usually spend their time in and how they use the space. For example, in a house where the family is more into the habit of watching TV together than reading books, the library may be the most untouched and therefore the one that's most likely to keep its organized structure.

The feeling you can glean at the end of tackling that first room will be the encouragement you need to keep going.

You definitely need those positive feelings when decluttering as it's inevitable that you will have to get rid of some things. Don't panic! Nobody is asking you to check your sentimentality at the door. It's completely normal to feel attached to one's belongings and keepsakes, especially ones that hold a special memory. However, it's just as important to make sure that these attachments aren't negatively influencing your well-being and the life that you have now and putting barricades in your progression, development, and success.

Again, having a strategy for this can help lessen the anxiety. Have three categories in mind: keep, donate, and throw away. Every time you pick up an object that you aren't sure still belongs in your shelves or containers, ask yourself if it's still of any use to you — whether physically (as in your everyday life and work), or emotionally (as in it gives you invaluable comfort and helps you keep a proactive state of mind). Separate these objects into three piles. Some of them add value to your life, and some don't. If they fall into the latter, consider whether they can still be donated so that others can benefit from them, or if they need to be disposed of already.

Always remember that starting is the hardest part. It takes discipline and a willingness to turn your space into a home in order to really put physical objects in order, but once that feeling of accomplishment begins to settle in your gut, you'll keep going because the rewards are worth it, and you deserve a home that allows you to be the best version of yourself.

Declutter your schedule as well. Make use of the concept of "clustering".

Declutter your schedule as well. Make use of the concept of "clustering" which involves grouping activities together based on the location or the task.

One thing you might not be taking into consideration when you begin the process of decluttering is time. Just as you value your personal space and your home, so should you value your time. It's something you can't get back if you waste it overcoming scheduling hurdles caused by disorganization, whether physical or mental.

Efficiency should not be applied only in the workplace. It's important to have that trait in the home and in one's personal life because it allows more room for things of significance — things that can add value to the overall scheme of things.

This is where the concept of "clustering" can really come in handy. Simply put, clustering is grouping activities — whether these are chores, events, or otherwise — together based on the location in which they are to be performed.

For example, if the kitchen needs a general cleaning, and there's a bake sale you want to participate in, schedule a "kitchen day." Bake the goodies first before cleaning the kitchen. This will allow you to focus on the pastries without worrying about making a mess. If you can throw in dinner preparations while the cupcakes are in the oven, do so!

After "kitchen day," you can do "living room day." If there are friends that you've been missing or a family gathering that you've been meaning to initiate, you can invite everyone over for a small party. Play boardgames in the living room, and take advantage of this time to catch up and bond with your loved ones. Yes, there will be a mess later, and as the gracious host you'll have to clean most of it up. However, look on the bright side! You can use this as an opportunity to do an in-depth cleaning, and if you've been meaning to rearrange some of your furniture, you can now do so. Vacuum the rug, reupholster the couch, repair the coffee table with the uneven legs — this is the time to do it.

Finally, you can set a "bathroom day." As with any part of the home, you want the bathroom to be a place where you can relax, where everything is in working order and in its proper place. You know the feeling of a long, leisurely shower at the end of a stressful workday? It'll be easier to achieve that if you turn your bathroom into an organized, efficient sanctuary. For bathroom day, think of everything that you want to do that's related to your bathroom, whether that's reattaching the fixtures or simply buying new toiletries. Buy everything you need, change into comfortable clothes, and begin cleaning. When you're done, take that long, leisurely shower, and enjoy the benefits of your hard work.

It's all about killing two (or more) birds with one stone. Clustering allows you to focus, as well as to optimize your efficiency. When you're not wasting time and getting frazzled jumping from one room to another, you're focusing your energy on the things that matter, and ultimately this will give you better results.

Recapping the major tenets of decluttering

1. Invest more in relationships than possessions. If you're going to spend extra money, treat someone to a meal at a restaurant instead of buying a new pair of shoes, etc.

2. Employ the 6-month rule to clothing. If you can make it half the year (two distinct temperature seasons) without wearing it, you might want to consider donating it.

3. Establish and enforce a proper "home" for what you own. The floor isn't a home. The dining room table isn't a home. A "home" is a logical place of storage or use. If something isn't in its home, address it quickly.

4. As often as possible, choose to "borrow" rather than "buy." This is particularly useful with books, but it can apply to other areas as well. The less you bring into your home, the less you will find yourself dealing with clutter.

5. Make ample use of "accordion folders" to avoid living in a disorganized world of paperwork.

6. One day each week, pick a room to organize and minimize. When you address what is in the room, organize it the contents into three containers or piles (1. keep, 2. donate or 3. throw away).

7. Declutter your schedule as well. Make use of the concept of "clustering" which involves grouping activities together based on the location or the task.

Notable Quotes for Inspiration and Motivation

"I have a notion that if you are going to be spiritually curious, you better not get cluttered up with too many material things."

- Mary Oliver

"There was a subtlety about Peggy Lee. It was powerful. There was a valuable use of space. Everything was not cluttered. Her voice was out front and was the key instrument."
- Rita Coolidge

"In character, in manner, in style, in all things, the supreme excellence is simplicity."
- Henry Wadsworth Longfellow

"That's been one of my mantras - focus and simplicity. Simple can be harder than complex: You have to work hard to get your thinking clean to make it simple. But it's worth it in the end because once you get there, you can move mountains."

- Steve Jobs

"Don't get me wrong, I admire elegance and have an appreciation of the finer things in life. But to me, beauty lies in simplicity."
- Mark Hyman

"The art of art, the glory of expression and the sunshine of the light of letters, is simplicity."
- Walt Whitman

"Science is organized knowledge.
Wisdom is organized life."
- Immanuel Kant

"Successful organizing is based on the recognition that people get organized because they, too, have a vision."
- Paul Wellstone

"Organizing ahead of time makes the work more enjoyable. Chefs cut up the onions and have the ingredients lined up ahead of time and have them ready to go. When everything is organized you can clean as you go and it makes everything so much easier and fun."

- Anne Burrell

"Messy stuff irritates me. I don't like messiness. If you leave something around my house, I'll tell you to move it back, clean it up, throw it in the trash - don't matter, just get rid of it. I need stuff neat, organized. And once I start cleaning stuff, I don't stop until it's done. Otherwise I'm irritated all day."

- Russell Westbrook

"Cleaning is my favorite way to relax. I clear things out and get rid of the stuff I don't need. When the food pantry and the refrigerator are organized, I feel less stressed."
- Jennifer Morrison

"When you say 'control freak' and 'OCD' and 'organized,' that suggests someone who's cold in nature, and I'm just not. Like, I'm really open when it comes to letting people in. But I just like my house to be neat, and I don't like to make big messes that would hurt people."
- Taylor Swift

"Be regular and orderly in your life, that you may be violent and original in your work."
- Clive Barker

Printed in Great Britain
by Amazon